City Pit

by Fred Mos

Memoirs of a Speedwell Miner

City Pit

by Fred Moss

Memoirs of a Speedwell Miner

Bristol Broadsides

Acknowledgements:

Thanks to:

South West Arts, Avon County Council, Access, Myna Trustram, Patricia Lindegaard, Ernie Ross, David Amos.

Produced by:

Bristol Broadsides (co-op) Ltd. 108c Stokes Croft, Bristol BS1 3RU.

Copyright:

© Fred Moss and Bristol Broadsides. (1986)

Printing:

Pressgang Co-operative Ltd.

Typesetting by:

JCL Graphics Ltd.

ISBN 0 906944 25 2.

More copies available from Bristol Broadsides at £2.50 (plus 60p p&p).
Bristol Broadsides is a member of the Federation of Worker Writers and Community Publishers.

Photograph Acknowledgements:

Thanks to John Podpadec who took the photographs on pages 1, 8, 10, 28, 45, 55, 56, 61, 63, 64, 66, 67, 70 and on the front cover.

We would like to thank John Cornwall for permission to reproduce the photographs and illustrations on pages 13, 17, 19, 21, 23, 24, 31, 32, 33, 34, 38, 41, 49, 50, 51.

Contents:

Introduction

Once upon a time, Bristol was a city of pits. Coal mining used to be an important part of the local economy and hundreds of Bristolians found employment in the industry. Fred Moss was a miner in the Speedwell Pit in East Bristol. He began work at the age of 14 just after the First World War and continued to work there until it shut in 1936. This book is his autobiography.

This is a unique record of the life of a Bristol coal miner. Fred vividly describes the very poor working conditions, the long underground walks to the coal face and the frequent accidents, some of which were fatal. He also writes about the mining communities and the strong bonds that existed between people whose incomes were very low and for whom life was a hard struggle.

Speedwell was the last pit in Bristol proper to close. There had been many pits throughout Bedminster and East Bristol. The Bedminster pits included - Dean Lane, South Liberty Lane and Malago Vale. In East Bristol there had been pits at Speedwell, Hanham and Kingswood. Many of the smaller pits stopped working in the 19th century. The larger and more profitable pits stayed open until the 1920s and 1930s. All the pits eventually shut, forcing miners onto the dole or into other work. One or two pits outside the City stayed open much longer. The Frog Lane Colliery, Coalpit Heath, closed in 1949 and Harry Stoke, a drift mine, in the 1960s.

There is still plenty of coal under the streets of Bristol but the seams were narrow, the rock formations faulted and the investments into the industry relatively low. When the mine owners were no longer making sufficient profits, pits were closed, shafts were sealed and equipment and buildings were dismantled. Today (1986) there is little evidence that Bristol was a mining city. The odd wall or building survives, there are miners' cottages still standing and there are a few miners still alive to tell the tale.

The miners of East Bristol had a tradition of militancy going back to the 18th century. At that time the pits were very small. In 1750 there were about 140 collieries in and around Bristol. Many lay outside the City Boundaries, but they had emerged in response to the industrial expansion of the period that had greatly increased the demand for coal. The miners of Kingswood, during this period, were regarded with some fear by City dignitaries. The Kingswood miners were known to march into Bristol when their interests were threatened, employing the only tool that working people then had for political expression - the riot. A major grievance was the turnpike which forced miners to pay a duty on the coal they were bringing into the city. Many a turnpike was destroyed.

It took a long while for the miners to form themselves into a union. Nationally miners were quite disorganised until the 1880s, with local organisations growing up in response to local disputes, then often disappearing. The peaks and troughs of the economy usually determined the nature of disputes. 1889 saw a general demand for improvements in wages and conditions - from all sections of the workforce. Many unskilled workers became unionised for the first time and it is no accident that 1889 saw the growth of the Miners' Federation of Great Britain the first genuinely national body which commanded the support of most of the local regions, including Bristol. 1889 was a period of economic upturn. With depression in the 1890s coal prices fell and wages dropped. The union shifted its attention to reducing hours worked by miners. Campaigns from the union led to the Eight Hours Bill in 1908. Miners now worked an eight hour day, (plus winding time).

There were tremendous pressures from the mine owners to reduce miners' wages. Much of the history of the miners' union, locally and nationally in the first part of the 20th century, is of struggles to stop wage reduction, culminating in the General Strike of 1926 which Fred Moss describes in some detail. In Bristol, these pressures were all the greater and union officials had a difficult job on their hands. The local trade union was the Bristol Miners' Association. With the closure of pits its membership shrunk and it found itself on the defensive, more often than not. Fred describes some of the battles and the union characters.

At certain times work was difficult to find for the redundant miners, but Bristol always had a broad industrial base, never relying overmuch on one or two industries, and miners could often find alternative employment when their pit closed, though many became unemployed.

The experiences of miners in Bristol during the 1920s and 1930s were not dissimilar to those of miners throughout the country in the 1980s. Then as now many were prepared to make a fight of it — against overwhelming odds.

The experiences of working, and unemployed, people are an important part of history. *City Pit* enriches our view of Bristol's past, exploring one of its little known aspects.

Bristol Broadsides will soon be producing a major series of novels and autobiographies by working people that will take this process a stage further. If you have a manuscript to submit, please let us know.

Fred Moss talking to Myna Trustram, who introduced the manuscript to Bristol Broadsides, about life in the pits.

Boyhood

I was born in 1906 in the east part of Bristol, Two Mile Hill to be precise; an area where coal-mines existed for many years. In this area, there were very many miners who worked in these mines. The Bristol mines were not very easy to work in, the seams of coal were small, sometimes only two feet thick, so that miners had to work kneeling and sometimes lying on their backs and their reward in wages was very poor.

I was eight in 1914 and I was now old enough to understand a little of how tough and difficult life was. It was the year of the First World War. My father, being a miner, was not conscripted to be a soldier; his job kept him out of active war service. The food prices began to increase but the miners' wages stayed low and did not rise with the cost of living. Miners' families went short of food. In some cases families had only one good meal a day, but some miners' families were better off financially so they gave some help to their poorer work-mates. The miners and their families were a closely knit community, and that still exists today in other mining areas.

There began an outcry by the miners and through their union voice they threatened to call a national strike if the mine owners refused a rise in their wage structure. The case went to arbitration, chaired by Lord Sankey, and the miners were awarded a wage rise. Basic rates were raised. Miners and their families were a lot better off financially but, through the rationings, people were still very short of food and clothes. Times were very hard with very little help from the remainder of the public. Many miners, particularly the younger men, decided that they could be no worse off in the armed forces and volunteered their services. Most of them joined the army, some went into the navy. Most of them knew of the dangers that confronted them but they were quite happy to get away from the awful conditions that existed in many of the collieries. Many were killed and a great many were wounded, but my father told me that some of the wounded men told him that they had no regrets in giving up colliery work for military service.

As for myself I accepted everything as it was at that time; poor food, poorly shod, and always wearing second hand clothes, but my family consisting of father, mother, three brothers and two sisters, were not miserable. We used to sing quite a lot. My mother was gifted with a beautiful soprano voice and she was a good pianist. We were all very hungry at times but happy.

The war had now been raging for a year. I watched as many thousands of soldiers marched past our house. I became very excited as they marched past singing war songs. I did not understand that most of them would be killed or wounded.

I was now nine years of age. I used to run errands for neighbours

Fred Moss's old school in East Bristol. 1986.

and fetch coal for them earning myself a few coppers. I used to borrow a hand-cart that would hold one hundred weight of coal; I went to Deep Pit colliery to get the coal. I also fetched coal for shopkeepers who besides paying me, also gave me a meal. I was being better fed than my brothers and sisters. The war ended in 1918 when I was twelve.

My father became very ill, he had some sort of blood poisoning. His body was covered in boils and it was impossible for him to work. His sick pay was very low, so my mother asked the church for help. The vicar gave her one shilling, the shilling did buy a little food. Some miners' wives found out about our plight, they helped by giving us bread and potatoes and cabbages. After about three weeks father returned to work so conditions became easier for us. Father decided that we were going to have to move to another house in the centre of Bristol (Penn Street) which is now called Broadmead. I was sent to Castle Green School and of course my brothers and sisters also went to Castle Green.

I was very surprised to see so many boys and girls went to school bare-footed. I was amazed to see so many children without boots or shoes. I felt rich and a cut above them because I was wearing a good pair of boots. A lot of the children did not go home for their 12 o'clock lunch. They were given 3d (1½p) by their parents to buy lunch in the cafe. The cafe owner supplied a bowl of soup, a slice of dry bread, and a cup of tea for 3d (1½p). Then a Lord Mayor's scheme was brought in to provide every boy and girl with boots, providing that their parents could prove that they could not afford to buy foot wear for their children. Some children still came to school bare-footed, but they were told that they must wear the boots provided through the Lord Mayor.

We lived in that house for about three months, then father decided that we would all move back to East Bristol so as to be near his job. We moved into a cottage in Whitehall Road, St. George. My brother, my sisters and myself were sent to Rose Green School; it was a very good school and I was happy there. I played for the school soccer team and it was a good team and we won most of our matches. They were very happy times for me. I worked on a newspaper round and the pay was pretty good, the only problem was, that I had to leave home at five a.m., check in the newspapers at a depot in Victoria Street and then start delivering the papers at six a.m. I got home about 15 minutes after eight a.m. I then had a bit of breakfast and went off to school.

There were two collieries only a short distance from Rose Green School, Deep Pit and Speedwell, and although I worked on a morning paper round I still used to fetch coal for people from the collieries. My mates and myself had played for hours on the surrounding slag heaps.

My father used to come home from his work at Speedwell Pit sometimes feeling very depressed; a miner had been killed, and other men injured through a fall of a roof. He told my mother that he would never allow a son of his to work in a colliery.

Now I was nearing school leaving age. Most children left school when they reached 14 years of age and I would soon be 14. I used to ponder over what job I could do when I did leave school. My teacher gave me a letter for my father to read, the teacher had written and asked father to let me carry on going to school, but my father replied that I would have to leave school at 14. I could then get a job and help supplement the family income. So the time arrived for other school mates and myself to leave school.

I would like, if I may, to refer to an amusing incident that happened in 1917. The incident is to do with coal mining at that time. There was a man whose name was Abrahams, he owned two donkeys and a two-wheel cart, and used to do a little light hauling for anyone. Amongst his jobs was to haul coal from pits, mostly for the miners who were allowed free coal, three hundred weight through the winter months and two hundred weight through the summer months. Only married men were allowed the free coal and Mr Abrahams used to haul miners' coal from the pits to their homes. The price of delivery was very small, between 6d (2½p) to 9d . The coal would be left outside the house until someone else carried it in.

One day Mr Abrahams was driving his donkeys and cart to do a bit of hauling for a customer. They had just passed St. George's fountain on the Kingswood side when suddenly the donkeys decided to lay down right in the middle of the tram track. Mr Abrahams tried to coax them to get up but they would not respond, the trams to Kingswood were held up, and also the trams from Kingswood to Bristol. This business went on for about half an hour, then four policemen arrived, accusing Mr Abrahams of obstruction. Poor Mr Abrahams was in a terrible state of mind, people were crowding around laughing and joking, but still no movement from the donkeys. The police decided that somehow they would have to unharness the donkeys from the cart and lift each donkey from the track to the side of the road. Unfortunately the donkeys were very dirty and greasy. The police were half afraid to handle them, but eventually they got them off the track, but their trousers and hands were very greasy.

Poor Mr Abrahams was threatened with all sorts of charges, but later on he went to St. George's police station and apologised for the trouble he had caused and the police agreed not to make any charges against him. Mr Abrahams was a very well known character in that particular period of time.

Miners in the cage at the pit bottom ready to go up. Frog Lane Colliery. About 1905.

Starting Work

In January 1921 my father took me to Speedwell Colliery to be interviewed by the manager, Mr Seymour. He was a very nice man and he told my father that I could start work on the next week.

I must admit that I did not like the idea of working in a mine, but unemployment was very high at that time so I had no alternative but to take the job. The day came for me to start work. I got out of bed at five a.m. I went downstairs and lit the fire and then called father. He came down and dressed in his working clothes and then at five thirty a.m. we both left home for work. Mother had prepared our sandwiches the night before and father provided me with a tin can that held about three pints of water. He also gave me a lamp made from a Brasso tin with a spout soldered to it. A cotton wick was threaded down through the spout into the can itself, then a special oily wax was pushed into the can, the oil would then soak its way up through the wick which I could light with a match. It gave a pretty good light. The Brasso can had a piece of metal soldered on the opposite side from the spout which in turn was attached to a crown of a bowler hat with the rim cut from it. A slit was cut into the crown of the hat to be able to carry the lamp while wearing the bowler.

Everything seemed so strange to me. I was amongst a lot of men that I did not know, but they were a friendly lot, and after a lot of bantering from some of them I began to feel a little easier in my mind. It was now six a.m., time for my first descent down a mine shaft.

The cage carried twelve men, six men on the top deck and six men in the bottom deck. Two men walked onto the top deck, then father and myself were the next pair to walk on the deck, followed by two more men so that I would be surrounded by men. I was in a sort of protective custody. The cage was pulled up to allow the bottom deck to be loaded. The safety gates were closed and then a signal was given to the engine driver to lower the cage to the pit bottom, and at the same time to bring up an empty cage for another party of men to be lowered into the pit. The cage seemed to drop like a stone. We dropped down the shaft at a terrible speed. My stomach seemed to leave my body as the cage dropped down the shaft, and then suddenly it was as though the cage was going back up the shaft again but we were only slowing down. We were very near the bottom. The safety gates were opened and I felt a little jittery when I walked out of the cage but with some encouragement and joking from the men I soon began to settle down. It seemed as though I had landed into another world.

I was told that there was a long walk for me so I followed a line of men who walked in single file. I could catch the smell of bananas and also the smell of oranges that someone was carrying. I asked father why the smell of these things was so strong and he explained to me that we were walking into a return air stream that had been travelling all around the mine workings and was now travelling toward the mine shaft so as to go up the shaft and then disperse into the atmosphere. Therefore the pit shaft was called an upcast shaft. The gallery or road we were walking through was about eight feet wide and about six and a half feet high, and it was very closely timbered. We passed some horse stables; they were white washed and looked very clean and comfortable for the horses to return to after their eight hours working shift.

We had now walked 1,000 yards but there was still some distance to go before reaching my place of work. We had reached the top of an incline and looking down it frightened me, as everything looked absolutely black. It looked to me like a bottomless pit, but again the men assured me that everything would be alright.

I sat down with the men a few yards back from the incline and I saw another winding engine. A miner informed me that within a few minutes a train of six wooden trolleys would be drawn up the incline. We would sit in these trolleys and then be lowered down the incline and men would get off the trolleys and disperse into galleries and into the coal-face. I got off at a gallery that was used as an air-way, and waiting for me was a man called George. He smiled at me and said, 'Now you call me George and not Mr.' George was a man who was responsible for the flow of air around the coal-faces of all the galleries.

I followed him through a long low gallery until we reached our destination. He was digging a way up through some old workings so that air could make its way up through to new workings of coal. My job was to get rid of the rubbish by loading it into a low wooden box-like container which was built onto four wheels. When loaded I pushed it along the rails for about 60 or 70 yards. I then unloaded it into some old worked out gallery. It was very hot. My shorts were very wet, my boots felt very wet. The sweat was running down my legs into my boots. It made me feel very upset and strange to think that I sweated like I did, George told me that I would in no way be harmed and he warned me not to drink too much, but to wash my mouth out with water, thereby saving my water, and by drinking less I would not sweat quite so much. I did follow out his instructions.

George was a man in his 60s. I worked with him for about a year. I was now feeling more confident in myself. My first week's wages worked out at £2 and two shillings (£2.10p). My mother gave me back ten shillings (50p) pocket money. I felt a little proud and happy being able to give money toward the upkeep of our home and I used most of my pocket money toward buying new clothes for myself. After five or six months of working in the colliery I heard the men discussing a reduction in wages and a possible strike. The miners' agent and other union officials argued with the mine owners against a lowering of the miners' wages, but without success, so the miners voted to strike. Mr Charles Gill was miners' union agent, and Mr Bert Crewe was the treasurer, they both spent long hours arguing with the owners but lost their fight.

It was my first involvement in a strike. I hardly knew what was happening. I know that I felt very sad that a strike would deprive me of having any pocket money and that I would not be able to give my mother any money toward the upkeep of our home. The strike lasted nine weeks, but I had only two weeks strike pay, about ten shillings (50p) per week. After those two payments I received nothing for seven weeks. Mr Gill did obtain vouchers through the Bristol Co-operative Society that could be exchanged at the Co-op Stores for groceries, and miners also went around houses collecting money for the striking miners families, but only the married men with young children were allowed to have a share of the money collected, other single men like myself received nothing.

I signed on at the Labour Exchange in Victoria Street, Bristol. The clerks told me that I could go to a school belonging to the Merchant Venturers. That School was in Broad Weir opposite Philadelphia Street. Other unemployed young men were there. They were not miners. I was the only one amongst them that worked in a mine. We were taken to a gymnasium in Victoria Street. It belonged to the Colston School, but we were allowed to use it. We were also taken to Muller Road to play rugby, and to the swimming baths. We enjoyed the two hours swimming lessons given to us. We used the Kingsdown Baths and the Jacobs Wells Baths. We were given a cup of tea and a sandwich on each occasion we attended the school, which was for four days a week, but of course no money was given to us. I attended meetings of the miners, but Mr Gill was despondent and he told the meetings that the mine owners were not in any way offering any different terms so he advised the miners to go back to work. What the owners wanted was for the miners to accept a reduction of an award of two shillings (10p) given by a Lord Sankey during the war years 1914-1918. That meant that every day a miner worked he would receive two shillings, if he worked six days he would receive twelve shillings, if he worked five days he would receive ten shillings (50p) and there was also a war bonus added to the basic daily wage. The mine owners also demanded that the war bonus should go, so after nine weeks strike the miners went back to work for a lower wage. When I drew my first wage it was £2 and two shillings (£2.10p) but when I returned to my job, my wage had dropped to just over a £1 per week.

So married men with families must have had tremendous drops in their standard of living. While on strike I had tried hard to get other work but without success. There were no jobs going. There was a great

Two miners undercutting at the coal face in Frog Lane Colliery about 1905. Conditions were not dissimilar to those found at Speedwell Pit.

deal of unemployment in 1921 so I returned to my job feeling sad and bitter. During the whole of the nine weeks strike, father, mother, my brothers and sisters and myself and of course other miners' families went desperately short of food and heating facilities. Those days are still very vivid in my mind although it happened over sixty years ago.

Learning the Job

I now had reached the age of sixteen, the year was 1922. I was doing all sorts of jobs. One of them was filling trams with coal, they held about 10 cwts. I worked with two other miners, they hewed the coal, leaving me to shovel it into the trams.

After I had filled a tram I had to chalk a number on it. Each gang of hewers was given a number so that the weighman at the top of the pit would be able to identify who and where the tram of coal came from, then in turn the weighman would enter the number on the tram and the weight of the coal in the tram into a register. At the end of the eight hours shift the numbers of the trams that had been sent loaded would be totalled up and sent to the office, the office staff would then check up on the amount of coal sent up to the surface of the pit by each individual gang. There were two coal shifts, a morning shift that started at 6 a.m. until 2 p.m. The other coal shift was worked from 2 p.m. until 10 p.m., but these times were in later months reduced by half an hour making an eight hour shift into seven-and-a-half hours. Men worked six days a week.

Pay day was on a Thursday. The men would queue up outside the pay office for their pay docket and wages. Each docket was for the two hewers. On these dockets, the tonnage of coal that was sent out by them was stated, including how much per ton they received and the full total of money they had earned. Of course the tonnage of coal sent up by each gang was for the week previous to the Thursday which was the pay day. Sometimes if the gang I worked with had a good week's pay, I would be given a few shillings extra, but if they had a bad week's pay I would only receive my age allowance which was not a great lot at sixteen

I was now learning how to become a responsible miner, becoming attuned to the dangers in a mine. However careful you were, something would happen, like a fall of stone. The stone would not be very large, but large enough to cut into your flesh; not always a serious cut. I did not take a great deal of notice of these small cuts, but when they healed I was left with a blue scar which I would carry for the rest of my life, and I have quite a number of them. I have in my life as a miner, lost quite a number of finger and toe nails through minor accidents. But of course the nails always grew again.

I was 17 years of age in December 1923, so I was now entering my eighteenth year in 1924. I was now becoming accustomed to the life of

A group of miners at lunch in the Frog Lane Colliery. About 1905.

a miner and the very hard work and the very bad conditions. The bad ventilation caused the air around you to be very warm; the sweat ran from your body in streams, filling your boots which you had to empty, or the sweat would ruin your boots causing them to fall apart. I stopped wearing the boots and worked in my bare feet. After a few days the soles of my feet hardened, and I felt a lot more comfortable not wearing the boots. I never wore boots again while working in the colliery.

Now I will name some of the men that I worked amongst. A lot of the men had nick-names. There was a man whose name was Arthur Heathoote, his nick-name was "Dry Bread." One day the men were talking about food and Arthur said that he quite enjoyed eating dry bread. He was never again called Arthur by his mates. The name of "Dry Bread" stuck. He was quite happy to be called by his nick-name. His daughter was a sergeant in the Kingswood Salvation Army and went on to win a very high position in that body. Another man, by the name of Angel, was nick-named "Bloater." He was a very thin man and his sweat glands did not work properly. He sweated in patches which in turn looked like fish scales so hence the name "Bloater." Another man by the name of Williams was nick-named "Chinker Williams" because he did have Chinese features, although there was no Chinese blood anywhere in the family.

"Chinker" Williams was a good watch and clock repairer, and he repaired many time pieces for his fellow miners. Some of the miners were quite happy to pay him for the repairs. Other miners were not quite so honest; they promised payments, but they never did pay "Chinker," so Mr Williams decided that he would still carry on repairing watches and clocks but after he had repaired their timepieces he would pawn them, so making sure that he was paid for his labour. He would then give the pawn ticket to the owner of the timepiece so that he could redeem the watch or clock. The miners thought it a great joke but "Chinker" always had the last laugh.

There were other industries in the same area as the collieries. There were quarries that were worked by men digging out the clay which in turn went through rollers that crushed clay or clay stone to a fine powder which was then sprayed with water, turning the powder into a malleable substance that could be moulded by hand into bricks of fine quality. There were two brick making firms, - Whites of Whitehall Road, St George, and Hollychrome of Fishponds. There was also Fussells of Crofts End, St George. Fussells' industry was mostly making roof tiles, both double roman and pan tiles, all made by hand. Most of these men who worked in the quarries and the men who made the bricks and tiles and their wives and children lived and fraternised amongst coal-miners. They shared their sorrows and their happy periods with one another, a truly remarkable race of people, helping

A candle holder used in the Bristol coalfield around 1910.

the unfortunate and ready to help one another when in trouble. Unfortunately those sort of people have passed on.

These other industries are mentioned because my experiences of colliery life in the 1920s and 1930s included the quarry men, the brick makers and the roof tile makers and their families. As friends and neighbours the coal miners and the above mentioned people were inseperable. They were as one big family.

I was now becoming an experienced miner, digging out the coal and making sure that I followed the safety rules. The pit props to the roof had to be their correct distances, and I tapped the roof occasionally with my pick. By listening carefully I could tell whether the roof was safe or unsafe. It is only by good training that you learn to look after your safety.

In 1928 we were still burning naked lights but we would, within a very short time, be issued with safety Davy oil burning lamps. Two miners working on the night shift thought of a way of digging out coal the easy, but very dangerous way; that was by placing a naked light near a large crack in the seam and igniting the gas in the crack which would cause a small explosion thereby pushing out a large amount of coal. That particular night there was a large accumulation of gas. The resulting explosion and fire burnt both men very badly. Fortunately there were men working nearby; they smothered the flames and called for help. A miner who was a proficient "First Aid" man treated the burns as best he could, and then the two injured men were rushed to Cossham Hospital where they remained for many weeks. After an inquiry by mining and government officials all naked lights were banned. No smoking of pipes or cigarettes was allowed and no matches could be carried underground. Men were searched before entering the cage and any inflammable materials were confiscated and the person reprimanded and warned that if he was found carrying matches again, he would be prosecuted, resulting in a heavy fine or imprisonment or both.

The Davey lamps gave a very poor light, but the miners became accustomed to working in the light they afforded; but through working in that kind of poor light some men contracted a nervous disease of the eyes, called "Nystagmus." After a few months of working with the Davey lamp there was talk of a new type of battery lamp.

The trouble with the Davey lamp was that one had to be careful not to knock it against the timbers too hard. If you did it would put out the light. If a tram of coal had to be pushed out to the end of the gallery you had to be very careful how you carried the Davey lamp. A strap was buckled around your neck so that you could hang the lamp on it, so carrying the light safely without knocking it against the timber

Peg and Ball Oil Lamp used in Speedwell Pit 1910-20.

Carbide Lamps used between 1910 and 1951 in the Bristol and Somerset Coalfields.

props, but if you suddenly stood upright, the lamp would burn your chest, leaving a blister that would be quite painful for a few days. I gave up carrying the lamp hung onto my neck and carried it by the hook in my teeth as did most of the men when pushing trams of coal. Carrying the lamp in this way resulted in your teeth becoming chipped and rotten. There seemed to be no end to the troubles created in a miner's life while working underground.

Later on electric lamps were introduced; a very much better light. A Davey lamp was always kept near, hanging within about ten feet of the coal-face, so that if a dangerous amount of gas was accumulating, the Davey lamp flame would show blue instead of yellow. The overman or boss would be sent for. He would know if the pocket of gas was dangerously high. Then he would order the miners to a safer area of the coal face, but more often than not it would be quite safe to carry on working in that particular area.

Whitsun

One of the greatest events of the year was the marching of a great number of children and adults through the main streets of Kingswood, and a large number included in the procession were miners and their wives and children. If the miners and their wives were not in the procession they would be watching their children marching to the sound of brass band music.

This event happened at Whitsuntide, usually on a Whit Monday. It was a Temperance occasion, representing a fight against strong drink. It was mostly organised by Chapel people; there were Wesleyans, Methodists and other denominations who would all get together for this marvellous Whitsuntide occasion. Each chapel would have its own banner carried in the procession. Some of the banners were very large and very beautiful. Some depicted bible stories, some had angels depicted on them.

A lot of the pictures on the banners were done in silk cottons and in beautiful colours. There was a friendly rivalry between each chapel as to who could have the best turnout. Zion church, near Soundwell Road, always had the best turnout, both in banners and in number of children and adults. At that time (seventy years ago) it was a very rich church. Most of the people who attended it were prominent citizens, people who owned shops, people who were owners of property, and employers of labour in the boot factories. Right up to the Second World War, the wives and the children of these men all attended Zion church, so the collection plates were always full to overflowing. Sunday services were always attended by large numbers of people and of course some miners and their families also went. Mostly Wesleyan hymns and prayers were carried out there. Of course other chapels had large congregations; efforts towards a successful turnout by these other chapels were marvellous, sometimes people would be overcome by the splendour of it all. It would be quite common to see people with tears in their eyes and quite a few people would have a fainting fit. The sheer joy of experiencing the wonderful music from the fourteen or fifteen bands helped to make a wonderful day out for the mostly working class people; Crofts End Mission Band, the Salvation Army Band, Evangel Band, East Bristol Band, Kingswood Reformatory Fife & Drum Band and other bands that made the Whit Monday a day to remember for the rest of your life. The processions would finish up in a large field for all kinds of sport and there would also be tea and buns for everyone. There was one field that was often used for these occasions; it was Greens field in what was called at that time (65 years ago) Blackboy and Trumpet Lane. All these events happened in a large mining community, so most of the miners and their families participated in those events. Manchester was another town that organised almost the same Whit Monday event as Kingswood.

On the Coal Face

In 1924 I was helping out on the coal face. I was taught how to work a seam of coal; I was working on quick pitch seams, the idea was to hew out one end of the coal face upwards, which was very hard work, but the effort was worth it. After one end was dug out a matter of about three yards, I was taught to work along the coal face so that the coal would fall away from me. I was also taught how to use a five feet long steel bar. By pushing the bar into cracks of the seam and heaving on it I could pull over five to six tons of coal without one bit of it hitting me.

I was taught other safety precautions such as how and when to erect timbers to the roof. The distances between each prop was between six feet and four feet. I was taught how to test the roof by tapping it with my pick. If the roof was unsafe it would sound hollow but if it was safe it would sound firm; you would develop an ear for these sounds as it could mean saving yourself from serious injury or being killed through a fall of stone from the roof.

Of course I was still only being paid an apprentice rate, which was very low, but I persevered and I learned quickly. The overman always made enquiries as to how I was progressing; the report must have been that I was a quick learner and that I would make a good and capable miner. I was soon to prove myself as such. Hewers of the coal worked in pairs, but if one of the men was an absentee, his place had to be filled by another man and on several occasions I was called upon to fill the absentee's place. Now most of these miners worked on piece work rates. They were paid a certain rate per ton that they produced and most of them picked up a good wage, but I only received, from the man I had filled in for, my own apprentice rate. This meant that, although the man had lost a days work, he had lost only part of his day's pay as I had kept up the days quota in tonnage. So you see some miners were not always honest in dealing with their fellow workers.

My father found out that I was being paid less than I should have so he approached the under manager (a Mr MacIntyre) but he informed my father that he could not make the miner pay me more as he had paid me my correct rate. But, he said that in future, my rate of pay would be raised to a coal hewer's rate. So I was on an experienced miner's rate of pay at eighteen years of age. I was the youngest miner at that time to receive the full rate of pay. I was then to work with my father at the coal face. At that time, he had been a miner for about twenty five years. We worked together for quite a few years and I received the same wages as my father, which meant that I could give my mother quite a bit more money for the house keeping. I bought my own clothes and saved a bit of money for the Bank Holidays, for there were not any paid holidays in the 1920s. My father's christian name was Frederick. He and I worked together for several months on the big run coalface which was quick pitch coal.

Galleries were driven into the coal face and our own was between thirty and forty feet in length, with a gallery above us, and in front our length of the coal face. The galleries were not all one long coal face; the first gallery was worked for a couple of weeks before the next gallery below was started. All this was worked out for safety purposes. Quick pitch was worked in a different way to flat pitch coal. On a flat pitch seam, a long face could operate allowing a large gang of miners to work together, but there were not many level coal seams in the East Bristol and Kingswood area.

Before any of these galleries could be driven into the seam of coal, a party of miners would work on a coal face of just a few feet wide, driving downwards following the pitch of the seam. After they had driven downwards for about forty feet the first gallery would be worked to the right or left of the incline. The miners were always working in water while driving down into the coal face. The pumps were kept working to keep the level of the water low enough for the miners to work. These men were paid extra money because of the very bad conditions they were working under; Speedwell Pit and Deep Pit were known as wet pits. There was always a large volume of water pumped out of both pits. One of the beam pumps operated from Duncombe Pit, situated at Speedwell Road, St George, opposite what is now Speedwell School.

Unseen Danger

My father worked for thirty-two years in the mines but in all those years he only suffered a broken nose, but my work-mate and myself faced death, and we were both very lucky to escape.

Fred Moss, 1986, outside Cossham Hospital where injured miners
from local pit accidents were taken. The building of the hospital
was funded by Handel Cossham who was a local pit owner.

My work-mate, Jack Price, and myself were working night shift, which was a coal producing shift. This night shift working replaced the afternoon shift which had now become a repair shift. The morning coal was from 6 a.m. to 2 p.m., the afternoon repair shift was 2 p.m. to 10 p.m., the night shift was from 10 p.m. until 6 a.m. next morning. Jack Price was a Welshman who had worked in the Welsh mines for many years. He married a Bristol girl and she and Jack set up a home near Merthyr, South Wales, but she longed to get back to Bristol. Jack managed to rent a house in Hill Street, a street that used to lead off Milk Street near the town centre. Jack and his wife then moved to Bristol with their two children. Jack applied for a job at the Speedwell Colliery, and was given one and I was to be his workmate. Jack was a very intelligent man, he read all kinds of literature and he could talk in great depth on a number of subjects. One of his favourite subjects was the nationalising of the coal industry.

Anyway let's get back to that terrible night when we were both very lucky to escape death. After all the miners had descended into the pit, the men would separate and wend their way to their different districts. There was the East District and the North-West District. I worked in the North-West District, with my mate Jack. In this North-West district there was a very long incline to descend before walking to our galleries. Two train loads of men had to descend this long incline, which was between 700 yds and 800 yds long so there was a wait of half an hour between first and second journeys of trains. I always used the second journey of trains.

Jack and I were working in a gallery where the air was very thin. We complained to the night deputy (John Jefferies) about it. Toward the end of our eight hours stint the Deputy came to our gallery and tested the contents of the air by lowering the flame in the Davey Lamp.

It registered a very dangerous content of gas, therefore we were both ordered to work in another gallery on the next night shift. We were both very relieved at his decision. The next night arrived and we entered the cage together. We were joking with the other miners as we descended the pit-shaft. My mate got onto the first journey to descend the long incline, I as usual followed him on the second journey, but Jack decided that he had to obtain our tools so that we could go to work in the other gallery.

Jack entered the gallery to retrieve our tools, but on reaching the tools he collapsed as the air was very thin and really foul. As I was walking down to join Jack, a miner rushed up to me and cried, 'Jack is dead and I cannot reach him.' He had tried to reach Jack but he had just escaped becoming unconscious himself. Now to explain to you what my feelings were is very difficult. In the first place if you are trapped by a fall of roof you may be pinned down by the fall of rock. The rock will pin your legs or arms to the floor causing you extreme pain and agony, and you can be conscious through it all while being rescued. What I am about to describe to you is something different.

The moment I learned of Jack's unconscious state, my first reaction was fear, a fear that made me feel sick, a fear that my workmate was dead. It was an awful feeling.

I rushed to the gallery where Jack was lying unconscious. Before entering the gallery I breathed deeply and held my breath until I reached Jack's body. I had only pulled him a very short distance when suddenly I could no longer hold my breath. I had to exhale, and as soon as I tried to breathe in I too became unconscious. I felt absolutely nothing; no dizziness, no shortness of breath, I just became unconscious. I could have died at that moment without feeling anything whatsoever.

I was dragged along by other miners to a place where the air was good. The men gave me artificial respiration for what they said was half an hour before they saw movement, my head moving from side to side. I was fighting hard to get air back into my lungs. It was as if a ring of steel was gripping my throat, the agony of it was terrible. I struggled and kicked but I was held down. I could hear someone talking to me from what seemed a great distance away, 'Fred listen to me, lie quiet, relax, you are going to be alright.' Eventually I sat up, and the other miners were very happy to realize that I would survive. Then I saw my workmate, he was still unconscious and looked absolutely lifeless. Miners were working on him; they never gave up for one second, miners were each in turn working on him, then, suddenly his lips moved. That movement made them work all the harder on him. They had been working on him for nearly an hour already when suddenly Jack broke away from the men and started running away up the hauling way. He was gasping and fighting to breathe when two of the miners rugby tackled him, and brought him down to the floor. They calmed him down, and in a short time he sat up and asked what had happened to him. Everything was explained to him; how I had tried to rescue him, that I too had become unconscious, so they formed a chain and dragged both of us from the gallery.

While all this drama was going on, our Deputy was looking very worried and upset. He knew that if any information was passed on to the management there would be an enquiry set up and that he would be severly reprimanded or perhaps lose his job. We should have been moved from the gallery several days before we were ordered out.

Now, at the time of this incident there were only eight miners including Jack and myself. We all made a vow to the Deputy that none of us would divulge to anyone else the drama that happened on that particular night and that vow was never broken. The Deputy wanted to take Jack out of the pit but Jack refused the invitation because if he arrived at his home early in the morning, his wife would become really frightened as she had continually begged her husband to give up work-

Deep Pit in the 1890s.

Deep Pit in the 1890s.

Speedwell Colliery in the late 1890s.

Speedwell Colliery in the late 1890

ing in the mine. So Jack sat in a manhole for the rest of night but I carried on working with some other miners.

I remember the area around Speedwell Pit as it was in 1916; there were many miners' cottages in the area and there were a couple of farms near the Speedwell Colliery. The colliery was surrounded by fields except for the enormous slag heaps that buried the fields on the north side. They were ugly to look at, but they were accepted by the people as a necessary evil.

The miners and their families and other people as well, knew that the colliery was a place of employment, so however ugly the scene there were wages to be had, however small, to help feed their families. There was also a quarry nearby (Hollychrome Brick Co). The firm employed quite a large number of men, and of course coal was obtained nearby, so as to fire the bricks. It was a large quarry, but now it is filled in and the kilns and other buildings have disappeared; the slag heaps are gone as well. There were many miners' cottages near the Speedwell Pit but the majority of them belonged to private landlords, the colliery owners did not own many cottages in that area. There was one rank of miners' cottages in Rodney Road that could be reached by walking through a lane called Colliers Alley. This lane ran from Speedwell Road to Rodney Road, and was a few yards above the pit yard entrance on the opposite side of the colliery yard. There is a fire station built in the old pit yard and other parts of the yard are let out to other business operators. There are still about three or four cottages standing just above the old colliery yard. One of the farmers who owned the farm near the pit was a Mr H. Moss. He owned several butchers shops, and kept quite a few pigs on his farm; of course, as you already know, farmers could kill their own pigs and cattle in those days.

Now we will leave the Speedwell area for the time being and go to the parent colliery, Deep Pit. Speedwell and Deep Pit Collieries were owned by Sir Frank Beauchamp. Sir Frank was a Somerset man and he owned a number of the Somerset collieries. A Mr Seymour was the manager of both the Speedwell and Deep Pit Collieries. There was quite a considerable number of cottages and terraced houses near Deep Pit. There was an engineering firm (Messrs Pecket) nearby, also two quarries. At Fussells Quarry roof tiles were manufactured, double roman tiles and pan tiles. Of course there may have been other types of tiles made there, they were mostly hand made, there was not much machinery used then. The other quarry (Whites Quarries) were manufacturers of the famous wire cut brick, a very fine brick that was used for public buildings. Their second quality brick were mostly used in the building of houses. Whites also manufactured tiles, so you can visualise that it was a very busy area in respect of the creation of jobs for people living there and of course from surrounding districts.

Deep Pit was a lot shallower than Speedwell Pit, a difference of 200 or 300 feet. Speedwell shaft was 340 yards deep. Deep Pit shaft was between 250 and 270 feet deep and there were more than a 100 more men employed at Speedwell Colliery than at Deep Pit Colliery. The coal brought up from both the collieries was not really of good quality. After the burning of the coal there was left a lot of ash and dust, leaving domestic fire grates very dirty and it also created a lot of soot in the chimneys. Factory owners also complained of its dirty nature, but both pits continued to work full time for many years. Near the Deep Pit Colliery there was what was called "The Coke Ovens." Small coal was trucked to the coke ovens, and it was then taken through a washing by water process. All the coal would float on top of the water and any rubbish would sink to the bottom. The cleaned coal would go one way and rubbish would carry on by conveyor belt to be trapped into a truck which would be carried away by rail and tipped onto the slag heaps, of which there were many acres. The washed and cleaned coal would be tipped into retorts and burnt at a chosen temperature to be turned into a kind of coke. The coke was delivered to iron foundries to be used for smelting purposes. Great temperatures could be created by using this particular kind of coke. That also is a thing of the past. As you may know, electricity has taken the place of coke.

There was a beam pump nearby that was used to pump the water out of the Deep Pit workings. This beam pump like Duncombe Pit beam pump operated over the top of deep shafts so that the steel pipes could go right down to the seat of the water. Now, surrounding this Deep Pit pump, there were many areas of slag from both colleries and a great deal of rubbish from the coke ovens, and amongst these slag heaps there were cottages where some of the miners lived with their families. Old stone-built monstrosities, they were very damp, and breeding places for rats. The people complained about the conditions relating to the cottages, but not a great deal was done about it. What was so amazing, although the conditions were terrible, the people themselves were very cheerful and the men with their wives and children lived a happy family life. The children were always kept clean and although they were poorly clothed they always looked and smelt clean; the women always trying to look happy and always wearing a white calico pinafore. There was a blessing for all the married miners, they were allowed free coal, three hundredweights in the winter months and two hundredweights in the summer months.

There was another row of miners' cottages in Knapps Lane, a turning off Deep Pit Road. These cottages had great slag heaps in front of them which were two or three times higher than the cottages. The only protection that kept the slag heaps sliding onto the cottages and burying them, was a great stone wall. I can assure you that it was a very depressing sight especially on dark wet days. There was a tunnel under the slag heap that did allow miners to take a short cut to the Deep Pit Colliery. While I am ruminating about the Deep Pit area, let me tell you about "The Long Bar." This consisted of a lane running from Deep Pit Road to Holly Lodge Road. There were just a few houses in Holly Lodge, only a couple of miners lived there. Now about half way up this lane there was a pond called the "Lilly Pond." It was a pool consisting of water pumped from the nearby pit. In this lane there was also a single railway track, which was used to carry trucks of coal from Speedwell Pit to the main Great Western Railway line and of course the Midland Railway line. The track was also used to take trucks of small coal to the coke ovens and washing plant.

Now, near this lane there was an off-licence beer house. The afternoon shift miners would buy beer at this off-licence and on a nice sunny day would go to this lane and have a chat and a drink before descending the pit (Deep Pit). There would be twenty or thirty men either sitting on a grass bank or leaning against a wooden fence drinking and chatting before working and when the morning shift came up from work, some of them would buy a drink and stand or sit in the lane before going home. Yes! I would say that it was the longest bar in the world.

A Fatality

I shall be returning to Deep Pit later on. Now I must return to my years of working in Speedwell Colliery. Father and I were mates at the coal face. We were both working in the "Five Coals Seam." It was a soft coal and easy to work. In the seam itself there was a four to five inch thick seam of soft stone. This stone was on top of a two foot thickness of what was called bottom coal. We hewed out the soft stone to a depth of two feet. This was thrown back into the waste, which was called the "gob." This name applied to only Bristol Colleries.

It was now summer and the year was 1925 and I was still working on the "Five Coals Seam" with my father. At this particular time a new seam of coal was being developed called the "Big Vein." An incline had to be driven down to this new coal seam. The incline was very steep as the new seam of coal was well below the "Five Coals Seam," so each district had to be supplied with trams. This operated by alternately supplying one train of trams to the "Big Vein" and the next one to the "Five Coals Seam." When the train of trams were lowered into the "Five Coals" there was about seven or eight yards of slack steel rope to be pulled in as the run into the "Five Coals" was very flat. A young man was employed to pull in this slack towing rope, one inch and a quarter thick, and it was then hitched onto a train of eight loaded trams. The young man's job was to make sure that the slack rope did not tangle as the engine winding machine pulled it in. It was quite a dangerous job. After the train of loaded trams was being haul-

Hanham Colliery Rescue Team 1910-20. All of the local pits including Speedwell had their own colliery rescue teams.

ed up the incline the young man's job was to change the points so that the returning journey would descend onto the "Big Vein." His name was Joseph Hyman, a very nice, quietly spoken young man. He was a slimly built lad, only about five feet seven inches. Now, he had carried out this job for a number of months. Quite close to where he changed the points, there was what was called a "manhole." This was a cavity hewed out of the side of the incline, a place of safety to jump into for emergency purposes. One day Joe had turned the points when seven of the loaded trams became unhitched, leaving just one loaded tram on the end of the towing rope. There was always a man riding on the front of these trains and the sudden breakaway of these seven trams caused the remaining tram to spring suddenly many feet up the incline; the rider hung on grimly, thereby saving his own life. He was a very lucky man to stay alive. His name was Walter Fry and he lived at Staple Hill.

Before Joe could get into the "manhole" the trams piled on top of each other with Joe Hyman trapped underneath. There was nothing we could do to get the trams off his body. That had to be left to a rescue party. The accident caused the two districts to stop working. Every man was ordered to leave the two districts and climb the incline. There was no way that we could ride up the incline as usual. The awful thing about it all was that every man had to stand on Joe's body so as to climb over the tangled wreck of trams. I felt rather sick after the experience of standing on his body. It was a very long climb up the incline. You had to pull yourself up by hanging on tightly to the steel rails. The incline was very steep and it took about three quarters of an hour to get to the top of it. We walked through a gallery two or three hundred yards long to another incline, but the men could have a ride up this one. By the time we had walked to the pit shaft it had taken us over two hours. All the rest of the miners stopped work in sympathy. It was the custom in those days that all the men would stop work if there was a fatal accident.

Joe Hyman's mother was a widow, her husband had died in hospital after a colliery accident. Joe was the main breadwinner of the family after his father died, so one can imagine the awful shock that Mrs Hyman must have suffered on hearing of her son's death. All sorts of people tried to comfort her. The shock made her very ill and she remained bedridden for several days. You could see people everywhere talking about the accident and talking almost in a whisper as they fully realised the tragedy of it all. They were all so concerned about Mrs Hyman and how she was going to manage to feed the rest of the family without Joe's wages. She received quite a lot of help from people living near her and from people that lived some distance away in mining areas. To people in other areas it was just news; they were not greatly concerned.

The coroner at the inquest on Joe's accident brought in a verdict of accidental death, but strongly recommended that all couplings that joined one tram to another should be regularly examined. That I am afraid was only a matter-of-course judgement as examination of couplings were subsequently not always regularly carried out, but of course there was a sort of cursory examination at set periods. A close examination would interfere with the output of coal.

Mrs Hyman lived at the lower end of Plummers Hill and not far away was Crofts End Road where there was a Chapel called Crofts End Mission, which was always supported by mothers and fathers and their children. It was a very bright and happy Chapel to attend. Mr George Brown was the local preacher. His brother-in-law, a Mr Coles, helped to organise events such as concerts, Sunday schools, a choir and there was also a band. A marvellous band it was too. Of course the band is still in existence today. They (Mr G. Brown and Mr Coles) were helped by their wives and also by a Mr John Jefferies. All the men I have mentioned above, were miners. Mr Brown was a very highly respected man, very kind and pleasant. Besides having to work very hard in Deep Pit, he also worked very hard in making sure that his chapel was a happy place to be in. He also visited the sick people in his area. Any problems that people brought to him were examined thoroughly before he gave an answer as to whether he was capable of solving them. If he could not solve the problem for them he would always be able to recommend them to someone who could. He was a pious man but not narrow minded. He believed in Christ and his teachings, but he never taught anyone to fear Christ. He always preached as to how people should learn to love Christ.

To return to what happened at Joe Hyman's funeral. Mr Brown officiated. That particular day it was sunny and warm. Crofts End Mission was packed to overflowing. There were hundreds of people lining the pavements outside the Mission. Everyone looked so sad; yes there were plenty of women crying quite openly and unashamedly. Inside the Mission Mr Brown was speaking from the pulpit (I was in the Mission myself). It was a very comforting speech but when he was describing what sort of character Joe had, he broke down and he had to give up talking for a minute or so. Mr Brown knew Joe very well as he was a member of the Mission.

The coffin was placed on trestles directly under the pulpit; everyone in the mission could view it. Running around the mission hall there was a gallery that was also full of mourners. With the service over, the coffin was carried outside and placed into the hearse. Everyone slowly filed out of the mission behind the coffin. The hearse carrying it moved slowly on followed by two horse drawn carriages holding Joe's relations and of course his mother. A large number of people followed the funeral and saw Joe placed to rest at Greenbank Cemetery. After-

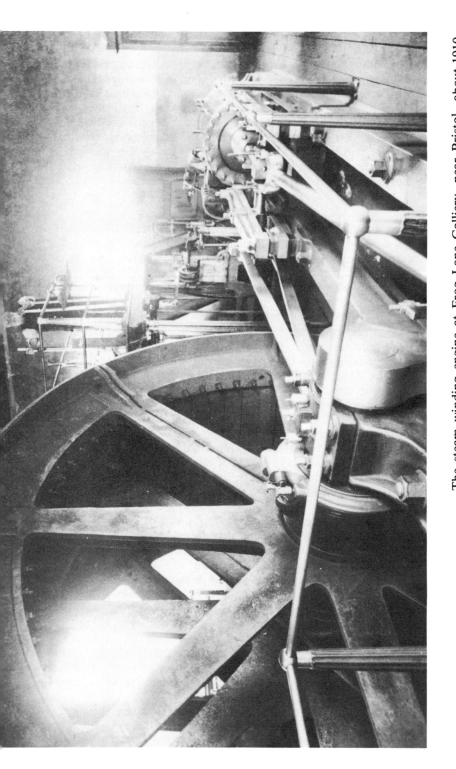

The steam winding engine at Frog Lane Colliery, near Bristol, about 1910.

wards there were a lot of arguments over what Joe's mother should be paid. Some people argued that Mrs Hyman should not be paid any compensation. As Joe was a single man, the mine owners were only liable for funeral expenses. Others argued, successfully, that Mrs Hyman depended upon her son's wages as the chief breadwinner and she received the sum of £350. Even so the Poor Law authorities tried to have part of the £350 paid over to them as they had paid Mrs Hyman money from Poor Law Relief, but I am happy to relate that they did not receive any of the £350.

Trade Unionism

At that time there were rumours of trouble breaking out again between miners and mine owners. The mine owners wanted new agreements worked out between the miners' unions and the mine-owners. The new pay agreements would mean a lower wage scale. These talks started in the year 1925, but there was no agreement. A national miners' strike took place in early 1926.

I will try and offer an insight into how the trade union of the Bristol East miners operated. When I started work in Speedwell Colliery, there must have been about four thousand miners affiliated to the Bristol trade union - the Bristol Miners Association. Mr Charles Gill was the Agent for those miners. The weekly subscription for each miner was one shilling (5p) per week but teenagers (14/16 years) only paid sixpence (2½p) per week. At the age of 16 you had to pay the full one shilling (5p). I was given to understand that the union was supported by the miners one hundred per cent.

From the time I joined the union in January 1921 until the 1926 General Strike, there was a state of outright friction between the colliery owners and miners over wages. The union was supported, sometimes by over-crowded meetings, and sometimes by very few members.

The union meeting rooms were at the end of a lane in Two Mile Hill, St George. The lane runs alongside St Michael The Archangel. The church is on the corner of The Kingsway which at the time I am writing about was named Cuckoo Lane.

The miners elected men to serve as delegates or miners' officials on committees or delegations to argue with mine-owners on any serious matter that could arise regarding wages or schemes that could be used to get a better output. The collieries I am referring to are Speedwell, Deep Pit, and Parkfield. Men from each colliery would put their names forward to serve as delegates or card stewards at the union's committee meetings, but there was also a miner who would put his name forward to serve as treasurer for the union (a very responsible job indeed).

The problem was, that very few miners would attend these meetings to elect the best men to serve on the union when needed. Anyway, two men from each colliery would be elected by a show of hands. In respect of the election of a treasurer, more serious thought was given. He had to be honest, a clever man with figures and also able to give a speech on all sorts of subjects concerning any difficulty that could arise between employer and employees. The man who was elected to serve as treasurer would work closely with the Miners' Agent, (Charles Gill). A Bert Crewe was elected to serve as treasurer.

He was the ideal man for the job. Bert Crewe and Charles Gill worked very well together. Union meetings were arranged at the end of every quarter of the year, but very few miners would attend these quarterly meetings. Some of them at the pit-head would grumble at certain things not carried out at the quarterly meetings. When they were asked if they had attended the meetings they would shuffle their feet and try to make an excuse why they had not attended, and then they would be told off in no uncertain terms. I attended nearly all the meetings as I was always willing to learn how unions were organised and run and to what purpose our weekly subscriptions were being used. I was absolutely fascinated by some of the things I learnt.

I learnt that unity was strength, and that disunity was to border on defeat and an absolute loss of what you may be fighting for. I was concerned in three local strikes not including the "General Strike." Each of the three strikes were brought about by the local coal owners wanting reductions in our wages. The Bristol Miners' Union fought 'tooth and nail' against lower wage structures, but the miners were always the losers. On these occasions the meeting hall was packed by miners to overflowing.

Charles Gill was a great fighter for the miners' cause. On any delegate meeting with the employers he could put forward hard facts on why the miners were on strike; unfortunately all his arguments fell on deaf ears. There was only one thing that Mr Gill could do. He would call a mass meeting and recommend a return to work on the employers terms. The men would vote to continue the strike, although they were right down on the 'breadline.' Their wives were quite prepared to support their men although food was scarce and the children needed footwear and new clothes, but Mr Gill would, in the end, win the men over to go back to work. During the strike Mr Gill would organise house to house collections so that miners' families could get a little extra food.

There were two local strikes before the 1926 General Strike, and in 1928 there was another local strike against still lower wages. The basic wage was now down to just over five shillings per day (25p) but of course if you were on piece work on a good working coal seam you could double your basic wage. Mr Gill was always praised by the miners for his hard bargaining with the employers and no-one ever condemned his efforts in trying to make the miners lot an easier one.

Mr Gill was living in the Chessels part of Bedminster. The whole family were highly respected by everyone living in that area and of course by many more people living in Bristol.

He was elected to serve on the Bristol Council as a Labour Member. He served quite a large number of years, was made an Alderman and later he was elected to serve as Lord Mayor of Bristol. He rose from a working miner to a Lord Mayor. I think that was a wonderful experience for his family and also for himself.

The General Strike

Before writing about 1926 and the great "General Strike," I would like to explain how coal was being replaced by other types of fuel.

One of the first firms to start using a different kind of fuel for their furnaces was Frys, the chocolate making firm in Bristol. There were coal burning boilers in the Pithay leading off Wine Street, in 1918. I used to deliver morning newspapers to the boiler men. There were about five men feeding the fires with coal that heated the water contained in the very large boilers into steam. The steam was pumped around the many buildings near Fairfax Street and Union Street. It was used to operate the large number of machines necessary to the making of chocolate and cocoa. The old coal burning furnaces were taken out and replaced by ones which burned oil.

A remarkable change came about in the state and inside look of the building housing the boilers. Before there were large heaps of coal and heaps of clinker and ashes raked out from the furnaces. There was an enormous amount of dust filling the whole of the boiler house. It was a filthy place to be in at any time. With the oil fed furnaces the change was dramatic. Instead of dust and dirt there was cleanliness, and instead of fifteen or sixteen men working in the boiler house over the three shifts the number was reduced to two men on each of the shifts. The floor of the boiler house was kept very clean, a white line was painted on the floor about five feet from the furnaces and the boiler men were very happy about the change. Other industries changed over to oil burning furnaces.

Although I was young I could see and understand that less and less coal would be needed, therefore the number of working miners would be reduced, which in later years turned out to be correct. In those earlier years there were one million and a quarter miners employed in Great Britain, compared to less than half a million now.

The mine owners and the miners' union officials were in consultation all through 1925. The mine owners insisted that mine workers must accept a reduction in wage rates, because other types of fuel were being used in all kinds of industries and that less coal was needed because of the uses of other fuels. They argued also that coal was be-

A row of miners' cottages 1986. Speedwell miners lived in these cottages. The father of the man in the second doorway worked in the pit.

ing imported and sold to industry at a cheaper price than English mine owners could sell it at. The union officials argued that the mine workers were already receiving low wages and could in no way accept a lower standard of living. Charles Gill was the Chief Spokesman at these negotiations. He was the miners' agent for all the miners in and around Bristol, which included Coalpit Heath and Parkfield.

Parkfield Pit was a sister pit to Speedwell and Deep Pit, and situated at Pucklechurch.

Mr Gill had worked as a miner at South Liberty Pit in Bedminster. He was elected to be the Bristol Miners' Agent after the death of William Whitfield who was the Agent for a number of years. Mr Gill gave up his job as a miner and concentrated on union business, which was a full time job. He was a very learned man, he could negotiate and he was always sure of his facts.

The fight between mine-owners and workers went on and on without reaching any settlement whatsoever. The mine owners agreed that they were losing a lot of money each year and that they could no longer go on losing out in their profits. On the other hand Mr Gill argued that in no way would he advise his members to accept a reduction in their living standards.

So there was stalemate between the two parties. There was great unhappiness and a foreboding of what lay ahead for us miners. We could see that strike action was inevitable and the national miners' strike started early in 1926. There was very little money in the union coffers. The Bristol miners were paid two weeks strike pay, but Mr Gill organised a system of collection from the public. A group of miners visited houses carrying collection boxes and of course the collectors also carried a badge proving that they were genuine. They had to take a lot of abuse from some of the public, those people refusing to contribute to the miners cause, but the majority of people did contribute. The Bristol Co-operative Movement also gave great help. They had food vouchers printed, though of course they could only be changed at the Co-op shops. Married men with families to support would receive a higher value food voucher than a single man. I, being a single man, only received an eight shilling food voucher. The money that was collected was shared out to married men and their families, but single men received no money. It was a hard and difficult struggle, food was far from plentiful, children were given handouts in the way of clothes and footwear, free meals were given to the school children. The school fund did sustain the children but unfortunately it was not good food.

Sometimes they had a greasy sort of soup or fish, covered with a white sauce; sometimes they would get a mug of cocoa. The children ate these foods because they were hungry. Some children would not eat the food dished up by the school authorities, and they went hungry until they got home. The result was that a number of children suffered from rickets.

There was a Mr Wise who owned several butchers shops in Southville and Bedminster. He was a councillor on the Bristol Council, and he was also a great friend of Mr Gill's. Mr Wise gave away to the miners and their families many joints of meat and it was good meat too. I walked over to Southville from St. George to pick up the joints of meat given to our family.

I had to walk all the way there and back, there was no money available for tram fares. It was about a five miles walk to Mr Wise's shop and of course five miles back, but I was quite happy to do the journey. The meat went towards a good Sunday mid-day meal. We were lucky enough to receive several of these gifts of meat.

The strike was dragging on and on, the miners were bitter at the thought of returning to work and receiving less money for their labours. They were receiving a poor wage before the strike began and the thought of returning to work at lower wages made them more determined than ever to carry on. At the time of the miners' strike there was a Conservative Government in power. Baldwin was the Prime Minister. His sentiments were not for miners. In fact he was supposed to have made a statement saying, 'Don't promise too many meetings to try and settle the strike, let the strike drift on, starvation will force the miners to call off the strike.'

Now other workers were asking their union officials to call a strike in support of the miners' cause, that was how the great General Strike of 1926 came about. The General Strike lasted nine days, the rest of the world thought there would be an armed revolution, but good sense prevailed. There were scuffles in different parts of the country, but there was no Martial Law called for. Baldwin made a statement in Parliament that if the General Strike was not called off, he would have certain union leaders imprisoned.

A Mr J. H. Thomas, head of the Railway Workers' Union was the first union official to order his men back to work. A high proportion of railway workers were very angry with Mr Thomas for calling off the strike. In fact Mr Thomas was regarded as a traitor by other officials, and he was never again a popular man with other union officials.

A number of Bristol miners had built up small businesses. Some had small general stores that their wives would manage, bringing in an extra amount in profits that would help to subsidise the husband's wage. This in turn would give the family a better standard of living. There was one miner (a Mr F. Buck) whose wife built up a good laundry business (all washed and ironed by hand). Mr Buck's shop was in Chelsea Road, Easton. Some of the laundry had to be delivered to customers and Mr Buck after the strike used to deliver the laundry at night after he finished work. Mr Buck was the miners' chief-weighman. He was placed into the company's weighroom office to check on the company weighmen making sure that every tram of coal was weighed correctly. Mr. Buck was paid out of union funds for this job. He finished his job each day at four-thirty p.m. He would cycle home and have a meal and then he would start delivering the laundry to customers. He used a carrier cycle to get around on. Some evenings it would be ten p.m. before he finished his rounds, and he did this for many years. Another person (a Mr Cox) who worked at Deep Pit owned a small millinery business in Whitehall Road, St. George. The front parlour of their terraced house was turned into a small shop, and it was quite a thriving business. I will have a lot more to say about Mr Cox and his wife later on in my story.

Now back to the strike. There was one blackleg during the strike. He went back to work at Speedwell Colliery. He was escorted by two policemen all the way up Whitehall Road and Speedwell Road. None of the miners interfered with him, but women booed him all the way to the pit and there was always a very large number of women lining the road.

The police looked embarrassed. They could see how angry the women were; most of them were miners wives, but they never attempted to molest the blackleg or throw any missiles at him. I was there on several occasions when the women demonstrated against him. The blackleg carried on for a few days, but gave up as he could not stand the jeering of the women. I never found out who he was.

The strike was carried on by the miners although all the other industries were working and producing again. The miners were left to fight alone. The government had won the General Strike; it was indeed a very black outlook for the miners. Some of them worked on outcrop scams of coal. The Bristol miners produced a great deal of coal. There were plenty of buyers both for domestic use and for use in stoking the boilers of industry. These men were anxious to get money so as to be able to buy food and clothes for their wives and children. There was no Social Security in those days; there was the Poor Law Relief that was financed out of the rates, but if any miner or his wife approached the Relieving Officer for help they were very often offered a ticket for the workhouse. This would have meant splitting up of the whole family. In those days children would have been sent to one section of the workhouse, the women to another section and the man would be placed in yet another. In some cases the Relieving Officer would give a food voucher, but no money was paid out to striking miners by the Relieving Officer. Very often a miner who applied for help from these people was abused, sarcasm was thrown at them, the Relieving Officer accusing the men of depriving their families of food by refusing to work. Men would not argue in respect of the pros and

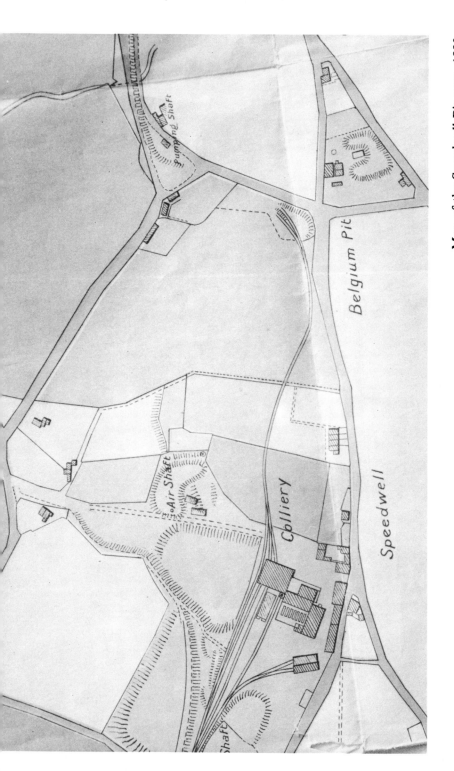

Map of the Speedwell Pit area. 1890.

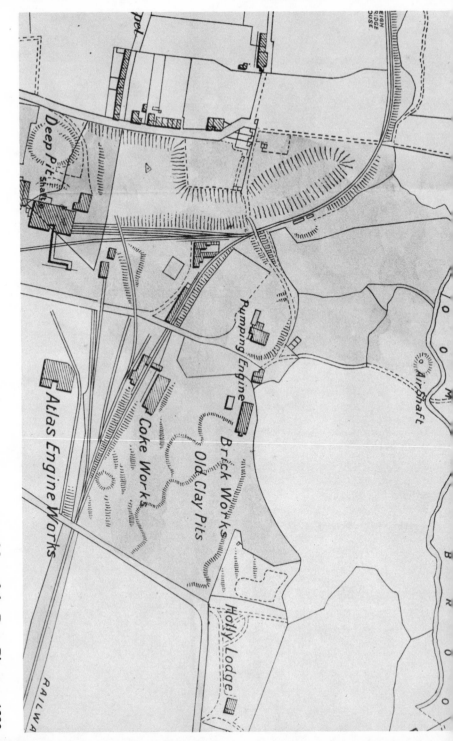

Map of the Deep Pit area. 1890.

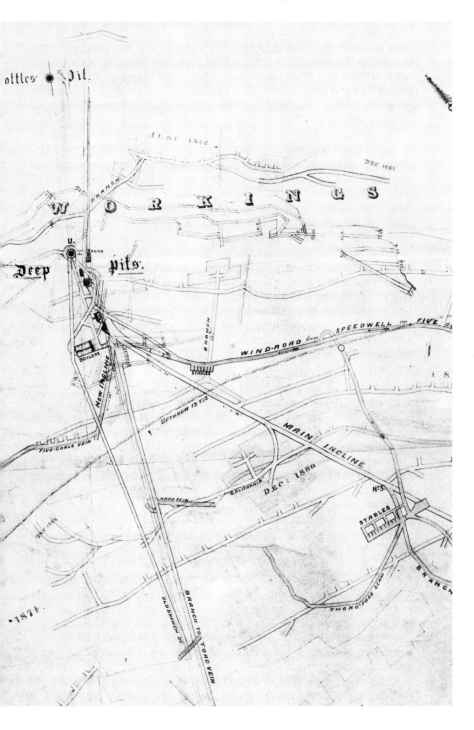

A plan of the underground workings at Deep Pit. 1880.

cons of their case, but they felt very sad about it all. The strike still carried on. Admittedly, the miners who were working the outcrop coal were not helping their cause, but who could blame them! It was a desperate fight for survival; their families needed food and all sorts of pressures were brought to bear by government and mine owners to defeat them.

There was, and still is, a great deal of outcrop coal in and around Bristol. There are outcrop coal seams at Coalpit Heath, Pucklechurch, Soundwell, and Fishponds. A great deal of outcrop coal was dug out near Cossham Hospital and Charlton Road. A large seam of coal s uncovered by quarry workers who worked in the Hollybrook quarry near Charlton Road, St George. The owners of the quarry applied to Bristol Miners' Union Officials for their permission for miners who were on strike to work the coal seam. The union committee gave their permission, so about eight miners were employed by the quarry owners. The miners were paid a good wage and of course the lucky miners were happy, the job lasted about three months. Troopers Hill in St George was another area where coal was mined. Troopers Hill at that time was said to belong to a Mr Ballard of Holly Lodge Road. He lived in a rather large detached house, partly surrounded by a large stable yard and stables. He also owned a lot of property in Bristol, much of it slum property.

Country Interlude

A workmate and myself were asked if we would care to go to Willsbridge. A Mr Cunnington had offered a home to two single young men. We both accepted the offer and we arrived at Mr Cunnington's house on a Friday. Mr Cunnington invited us into his house. He was a man of about seventy years of age; or older. He was kind and also a man with a very pleasant personality. He was an educated man and I like him straightaway but my workmate was not very keen to accept being in Mr Cunnington's care. I have quite a lot to write about Mr Cunnington.

The house was in Willsbridge Hill near the bend of the road that leads into Keynsham. It was a detached house, built with a double front. Two stone dogs were situated near the front of the house, a dog each side of the footpath. There was a very long garden belonging to the house; this was surrounded by a high stone wall. There were apple trees, pears, damsons, plums and all sorts of bush fruits, red currant and gooseberries. There were Victoria plums; the branches carrying the plums were trained along the stone wall. There were all sorts of vegetables growing in the garden and there were strawberries growing behind a small meshed wire.

The strawberries were protected on four sides and a wire mesh attached to side partitions, so protecting the strawberries from the top as well; as you may know all sorts of birds attack and eat strawberries when they are ripe.

I settled in very quickly but my workmate left and went home after a few days. He was not home-sick but he said that he could not adapt himself to the different kind of life. We read a lot as Mr Cunnington had a pretty large library of books and he encouraged us to read all types of literature. We helped out in the gardens besides meeting all sorts of people. Most of them were well educated and they used to ask us all sorts of questions. Where did we live? What kind of house did we live in? And most of all they were deeply interested in colliery conditions and how miners reacted to certain bad conditions, referring to the dust content, the bad air systems, the heat and what we wore while we were working underground. I gave them most of the answers. My workmate did not say anything. They were very kind people, and they looked on in disbelief when I explained to them what a miner's life entailed. Anyway my workmate returned home but I stayed on for quite a number of weeks. I certainly did not want to return home. Everything was so different from what I was born into. My very outlook on life changed. I was mixed up in something that I had not experienced before, good books to read, good food, a different sort of conversation to listen to. Yes, I was very happy that I had chosen to live at this house.

Mr Cunnington's father was a wine and spirit merchant. He was a very rich man, and a very successful business man in every way. Mr Cunnington had one sister and of course his mother, and the whole of the family were believers in the Roman Catholic faith or religion whichever word is correct. The servants were Catholics as well. Mr Cunnington's father would only employ people in his household who practised the Catholic faith. The whole family including the servants attended Mass regularly.

Inside the church everyone was treated and regarded as equal, whatever their station in life. According to Mr Cunnington, and these are his words as were spoken to me. 'Whatever is preached and carried out inside the church should be applied outside the church.' Mr Cunnington could not accept his parents attitude toward the servants. Inside the church the parents and servants were as equals, but Mr Cunnington and his sister were taught to regard the servants as serfs. Mr Cunnington could not accept his parents views, and he continued to treat the servants almost as part of the family. He quarrelled with his father over the treatment of the servants, resulting in his departure from home.

Now Mr Cunnington was quite able to look after himself. His parents had ensured that both the children had a good education so with his education and an allowance from his father, Mr Cunnington studied politics. I must state that the above events happened in Bournemouth.

Mr Cunnington came to Bristol and bought the house at Willsbridge. He was always on hand to help the underprivileged. What his politics were I did not know. He could have been a Socialist or a Liberal, but definitely not a Conservative. He told me that he had renounced the Catholic religion because of what he had experienced in his younger days. Of course I listened to what he had to say, I offered no argument to his statements.

Mr Cunnington was very fond of swimming. I used to accompany him and we would swim in the river Avon near Mr White's house. This was well known in Keynsham and surrounding villages. Mr White used to allow campers to pitch their tents in his field. Mr Cunnington and myself would finish our swim and walk back to his place, then he would prepare a meal with vegetables taken from the garden and he would buy a chop that would be either lamb or mutton to go with the vegetables, but he would never make gravy to pour over the meal. He considered that the gravy interfered with the taste of the vegetables.

After we had finished up our vegetable meal he would serve boiled rice full of raisins. It was delicious, and we would finish up with stewed mixed fruit. The stewed fruit was served cold. After our meal we would go out onto the lawn, and both sit in deck-chairs. I would then read to Mr Cunnington. He loved me to read stories about India to him. I would carry on reading to him for about an hour. He would then fall asleep and I would wander off and do a bit of gardening.

I met all kinds of people during my stay at Mr Cunningtons house. Pacifists, one man that was an out and out Communist, and others. The Communist fellow was a Welshman, a delightful man in that he was quite prepared to accept that there was a great deal of opposition to his way of thinking, but everyone in the room would listen to him and would not interrupt. On one occasion he spoke for two hours. There were about ten people in the room while this man was making his speech, including four people who lived nearby. These four people were really good friends of Mr Cunningtons. These were two men and their wives and the two men worked on the railway. While the speech was going on Mr Cunnington was preparing a meal for us all. He walked in from the kitchen and asked us to sit around the table while he served up the meal. That cut short the speech.

After we had finished our meal Mr Cunnington would invite everyone to a singsong. He would play the organ and we would all join in. He always played his organ according to his music sheets, he would never play from memory.

There was never a dull day. There was always something interesting to do. I helped to make one and a half hundredweight of jam, strawberry, plum, blackcurrant, damson, raspberry and gooseberry jam. There were two large copper pans that were used in boiling the

Fred Moss at Willsbridge 1986, outside the house where he stayed as a boy during the General Strike.

Fred Moss at the old tram track, 1986, opposite the Willsbridge house. The track went from the California Colliery to the river Avon.

fruit; one pan of fruit was allowed to cool, ready for placing into jars while the other pan was placed on the fire to boil and may I add that the fire consisted of tree wood. No coal was used while making the jam.

Mr Cunnington gave most of the jam away to miners and villagers. He was happy giving to people at anytime. The summer of 1926 was warm and beautiful, vegetables and fruit were plentiful. I helped in storing root crops for the winter, carrots, turnips and parsnips were stored away in wood boxes and covered in dried red sand.

We would rise at seven o'clock every morning, have a bath and then I would clean all the boots and shoes while Mr Cunnington prepared the breakfast which usually consisted of eggs and bacon, a mug of tea and finishing up with cold stewed mixed fruit. Sunday was a special day for me. Mr Cunnington always received invitations to give a speech at different chapels and churches. He was a capable speaker on all sorts of subjects, and he would always give interesting speeches. He was never dull. He would cycle to these different places of worship mostly going to afternoon services.

On one occasion we cycled to St Aidens Church, near Nags Head Hill, Bryants Hill, St George. At that time a Reverend Rogers was the resident vicar there and he organised what was called a working man's parliament. A room was set aside for men only. There would be a short religious service and then all the men would be allowed to smoke whether he was a pipe or a cigarette smoker. Mr Cunnington was invited to one of these sessions to give a speech. After he had given his speech, he would invite the men to ask questions. He could give a satisfactory answer to all the questioners. It was always a pleasant Sunday afternoon at St Aidens Church.

Week after week was rolling by and I was wondering when I would be told to go. I felt a little sad about having to leave and working again in the mine. I had been living there for eight or nine weeks and I had experienced a different sort of life, a life very far removed from working in a coalmine and the hard struggle to survive. While I was staying at the house I discovered an old tram track opposite, across the road. I walked along the track for a considerable distance, then I walked through a tunnel that also carried the tram track. I made enquiries about this track and learned that the track was laid down from the Californian Colliery to the river Avon in the nineteenth century.

The trams of coal were pulled along by horses to barges, into which the coal was loaded, to be carried to factories and other industries situated near the river in those days. Unfortunately houses are now built over the track.

Changes

The strike was settled. All the miners including myself went back to work on reduced wages. The mine owners had won after a very long struggle; nearly eight months strike by the miners had ended in defeat. Miners were forced to accept a lower standard of living. Community life amongst the miners and their families came back to life again, although wages were much lower, making it harder for families to buy enough food to feed their children properly. There was still that marvellous feeling of belonging to a community that was as one great family. Helping another family in distress was quite common in those days and no thanks were asked for. Families deemed it their duty to help one another.

There was a lot of repair to be done before coal could be sent out of the colliery. Some coal was sent out but it took some time before production could begin. The manager (Mr Seymour) was transferred to Parkfield Colliery, he had managed Speedwell and Deep Pit for many years. He was an excellent manager and all the miners were sorry to see him go. Mr Seymour was an expert in geology.

A new manager took over Mr Seymours duties The new manager's name was Mr Hunter. He was a man of tall stature. He was six feet two inches and he was also a largely built man. He paid a special visit to all the miners underground and introduced himself. He told the miners (including myself) that he had spent several years managing miners in China, and he told us that he was not happy with the conditions that Bristol miners were working under. He promised that he would have changes made, such as better airways and that the miners galleries would be made high enough for him to walk along with bending his body. He also told them that he had signed a contract of six months duration. The miners accepted him as a man who was understanding and sympathetic toward any miner who had a genuine complaint to make to him.

During the six months that Mr Hunter managed the collieries, the mine owners tried to induce him to sign another contract employing him for years instead of months. He would not sign another contract, but he did promise to carry on managing until they (the mine owners) could advertise for another manager.

During the time that Mr Hunter was manager, he took many photographs of men working at the coal-face, and of men pushing trams of coal to a base where they (the trams) would be hauled up an incline. Now all these were photographs of men working absolutely naked. It was too hot and dirty to wear shorts or shirts. The combination of dust and sweat sticking to the shorts or shirts would rub the skin off their bodies.

Mr Hunter's home was in Newcastle. He had a sister who also lived in Newcastle, the only sister he had. There were no brothers. He sent some of the photographs to his sister and she was appalled and upset at what she saw in them. She wrote a letter to her brother begging him to resign his job and come home at once. She could not bear to think that her brother was managing colleries where such terrible conditions existed. Everything I have written about Mr Hunter is absolutely true. He showed the photographs and the letters to the miners including my father.

The mine-owners advertised for a manager, and the advert was answered by a Mr Jones from Lancashire, who accepted the job. He must have signed a contract employing him for a number of years. Mr Jones was manager of the East Bristol Colleries right up to the time of closure. It was now 1928. The new manager was accepted by the miners. He was quite a decent man and he was fully prepared to co-operate with the miners in anything that was suggested by them to get a bigger output of coal. Mr Jones said he was employed to secure a larger output of coal and that he intended to obtain a larger output.

During 1928 there were several changes made in the running of Speedwell Colliery. First of all, naked lights were banned and Davey lamps were introduced. The Davey lamps were very poor compared to the naked lights which gave a much better light. The miners accepted the Davey lamps because several of their mates had been burned by small explosions caused by a build up of gas near the coal face. These Davey lamps were in use for a few months, and then wet battery powered lamps were introduced. These lamps gave off a beautiful white light. Although we had these new type of lights, a Davey lamp had to hang nearby, to measure any dangerous build up of gas. During 1928 the miners reached down to a big vein seam of coal which was flat pitch. This meant that the seam of coal was on a level surface different altogether to the quick pitch coal. On this level seam of coal, coal cutting machinery was used. The output of coal went up in a big way reaching a target that had never before been reached. Mr Jones (the manager) was delighted. His plans had paid off. Of course the miners were working behind the coal-cutting machine picked up good wages as they were all on piece work rates, which in those days were one shilling and eightpence per ton (8½p). These miners were very happy, but of course there were a lot of miners who could not get on machine-cut coal seams.

Another Accident

A miner by the name of Mr Cox had a wife who ran a millinery business from her home in Whitehall Road, St George. The front parlour was used as a shop where Mrs Cox built up a paying business selling lace curtains, elastics, little girls' dresses and all the paraphenalia attached to millinery. On this particular summer's day she decided to take her two little girls to Weston-Super-Mare. A couple of other mothers with their children went with Mrs Cox to Lawrence Hill Station and boarded the train for the sea-side.

Mr Cox was on early morning shift at the Deep Pit Colliery and he arranged with his wife that he would go to his work, promising her that he would leave his work earlier than usual, and after his bath he would catch the train to Weston so that he and his family could spend couple of hours together before leaving the seaside for home. Mr Cox did not reach Weston, he did not reach the top of the pit alive. Two men were at fault, Mr Cox arrived at the bottom of the shaft, during a period in which trams of coal were being hauled up the shaft. There are no safety gates used while coal is being hauled, and there are different signals sent to the top of the pit. There was a "knocker" signal that was operated by the banksman at the bottom of the shaft. He pulled down a wire that ran right up through the shaft, to an iron arm at the top of the shaft. This iron arm in turn would hit a round and flat iron plate. It was quite effective. The sound given off was like the sound of a bell. When the cage was loaded with two trams of coal a signal of "one" was pulled on the "Knocker." That was the signal to haul-away, but if men were loaded into a cage, safety gates would be attached to the cage and three knocks would be given to the engine driver. Now the terrible mistake that was made by both the banksman and Mr Cox, was that they both ignored the safety rules. Mr Cox asked the banksman not to bother about affixing the safety gates as he was in a hurry. The banksman allowed Mr Cox into the cage without the gates. He gave the signal of "one", and away went the cage with Mr Cox in it. After several journeys of coal had been sent up following Mr Cox's departure, the banksman phoned to the top of the pit and enquired as to whether Mr Cox had arrived at the pit-top. The message he had back was that no-one had come up the shaft. The hauling of coal was immediately stopped. There was panic and disbelief that anyone should and could break safety rules. All the miners were ordered to stop work, and find their way underground to Speedwell Colliery, where they would be hauled to the top of the Speedwell shaft. That meant a two hour journey for all the miners to get from Deep Pit to Speedwell, having to practically crawl in places. The search went on for Mr Cox's body; he must have fainted on the way up the shaft and must have been a considerable way up when he fell out. Parts of his body were found in the "sump" and it had been torn about very badly.

Mrs Cox went to the station to meet her husband, but when the train arrived he was not on it, so she walked back to the beach thinking that perhaps her husband could not leave his job early enough to bother about going to Weston.

She rejoined her friends and they were all very happy together. An hour or so later a newspaper seller approached them shouting 'Pit disaster in Bristol Coal Mine.' Mrs Cox bought a newspaper and in it was printed her husband's name. In those days victims names could be printed before relatives were informed first: today that would not be allowed to happen. After the coroners verdict (causes unknown) the banksman was severely reprimanded and he was very lucky not to be

The Mission. 1986.

CROFTS END MISSION.
FOUNDED 1895
BY
GEORGE A. BROWN.

charged with manslaughter. Anyway he was transferred to another job at Speedwell Pit. All the miners showed great sympathy for him. Not one man blamed him for the death of Mr Cox. Even Mrs Cox showed great sympathy towards him. She quite understood the circumstances that resulted in her husband's death. She herself was in a state of shock for a long time. Neighbours rallied around, her business was looked after, the children were cared for, her house was kept clean and Mrs Cox herself was given a great deal of care and attention by neighbours and relations.

The day arrived for Mr Cox's burial. It was again a beautiful summer's day. The pavements were crowded with people. The funeral cortege made its way up to Crofts End Mission where Mr Brown would again head the service. Mr Brown again broke down while giving a speech on the dangers of coal mining. There were a great number of people lining the pavements all the way to the mission hall and once again the mission hall was packed with people, sad in the knowledge that another life had been lost in the quest for coal.

These people were wonderful. They were sincere in their grief and had their wonderful spirit of togetherness. In sickness and in health, they were at hand to help any neighbour who needed their help.

Mr Cox was interred at Greenbank Cemetery.

The End of The Bristol Coalfield

The extra output of coal had been achieved and the manager was very pleased that this had been successful. A great deal of coal was brought by the electricity board but gradually the orders were getting smaller and smaller. Deep Pit and Speedwell Pit were put on short-time working; the collieries worked for one week and closed down for one week. The miners signed on at the Employment Exchange on the week they were off work. This operation continued for quite a number of months. Some miners who had passed very stiff examinations on shot-firing and also the correct safety procedures in the course of shot-firing, found jobs under the Bristol Corporation. The great storm-water project was in progress at that time, so a few of the Bristol miners and shot-firers were employed there. That project is still in progress.

Gradually the collieries were being worked full time, but the rumours were being passed around that the mine-owners were seeking another lowering of wages. The owners' argument was that competition from other mine-owners had to be met by Bristol owners lowering the price of coal, and the lower price could only be made by lowering costs which in turn meant the lowering of men's wages. Mr Gill our union agent fought hard against any lowering of wages, but the lower wage terms had to be accepted. The Bristol miners were angry and furious. The flat rate of pay was then one pound, 19 shillings and 10 pence (£1.98p) for six days work and one pound and seven shillings

The Beaufort Arms, 1986. Known locally as the 'Beat 'em and Whack 'em', the pub was the local for many miners at Speedwell Pit.

The Speedwell Colliery wall in Whitefield Avenue, still standing in 1986.

(£1.35p) for five shifts. Of course extra money could be earned if you were on piece work rates. Men would agree to a certain price per ton paid on whatever tonnage of coal produced. As before, some miners earned extra money but those who only received flat rates were made to struggle very hard to try and feed their families. It is a fact that their wages were below the subsistence rate, set by the Poor Law authorities. Some miners received assistance although they were working.

Of course this only applied to a family where a miner had a wife and three or four children to support. A miner with a wife and one or two children would have to manage on his low wage.

More and more miners were leaving the Bristol mines in the early thirties to find work in other coal mines, whose working conditions and wages structure were better than they were in the Bristol mines. Many of the Bristol miners went to live and work in the Kentish coal mines. These were more modern than the Bristol mines and there was good housing accommodation for their families. The wages were better and working conditions were far superior to what they were in Bristol. Miners could work while wearing shorts and flannel shirts because of the more modern system of airways. The air was pumped right up to the coal face making working conditions more tolerable and the air was very cool and not hot as it was in the Bristol mines.

There was a shortage of miners available for working in the Bristol mines. Men from South Wales and the Forest of Dean came to work in the Bristol mines, but many of them did not stay very long. After two or three weeks they would leave, the conditions being too bad for them. In 1932 I was beginning to realize that I must give up my job as a miner. Wages were poor and I was very unhappy with not being able to buy the clothes I needed. I could not afford to visit a theatre, I could not afford to take a holiday. There were no paid holidays for miners in the 1930s. I took a week off from work to seek other employment. I was very lucky. I found a job in the building trade. I started work without giving notice that I was giving up my job as a miner as there was no hard and fast rule about giving any notice. When I started work in the building industry, I was asked if I had brought along with me my insurance card. I replied that I would bring it along shortly. I was afraid that if I informed the foreman that I was already employed as a miner, I would not have been given a job. I was given a week to produce the card and I wrote to the office at the Speedwell Colliery asking for my card to be posted to my address. I duly received the card without any fuss or bother.

I worked on the building of a new retort house at Canons Marsh Gas Works. It was being built to extract gas and other by-products from coal. By working overtime I was able to pick up a good wage and I worked at Canon's Marsh for about ten months. I was sacked about two weeks before Xmas 1932. I was signed on at the employment ex-

Fred Moss 1986, standing in front of where the Speedwell pit-head
building used to be. The pit closed in 1936.

'That was where the pit-head was.' Fred Moss at Speedwell 1986.

change, in Victoria Street, near Temple Meads Railway Station. When the clerk found my file he found that I was an experienced miner. Straightaway he gave me a green card and directed me to go to Speedwell Colliery as they were in need of miners.

I went to the colliery as ordered. I was directed to the manager's office and he was very pleased to see me, but when I asked him to write on the card that I was not suitable for the job, he became very angry so I also became angry and walked out of the office. I went back to the Labour Exchange and told the clerk that I had refused the job. I received about two weeks employment pay and then had to appear before a tribunal and explain to them why I had refused employment. My explanation did not satisfy them, so I was refused employment pay for six weeks. I managed to get through that six weeks, determined that I would never again work in a colliery.

Unemployment was very high in and around the Bristol area in the 1930s. Collieries were being closed down, boot and shoe factories were either operating on short-time or had stopped producing and had closed down, never to open up again. A large house-building programme was in progress from the late 1920s to the late 1930s. A large number of men were employed in the building industry, but a very large number were still without employment. The community accepted the conditions in what I can only describe as a fatalistic manner. They could still have a joke and would offer a helping hand to anyone that needed help.

Speedwell Colliery continued producing coal until 1936. That colliery had produced coal for almost 100 years.

In 1935 the mine owners decided that the Speedwell Colliery was to close, but the Lord Mayor at that time set up a public fund so as to keep the colliery open and keep the men employed as unemployment was very high. The public responded by building up a fund of between £3,000 and £5,000. This money was passed over to the mine owners to be used in searching for and developing a new seam of coal. The money was used to keep the Speedwell Colliery working for just one year, after which it closed down. Deep Pit Colliery closed a bit later on followed by Parkfield 1936 and then Coalpit Heath in 1949. So the coal producing area of Bristol East had finished for ever, except for the Harry Stoke Colliery which closed in 1963. It was what is called a "Drift Mine." Instead of a mine-shaft an incline was driven down to the coal seams. That meant that only shallow seams could be worked. The good seams were at a greater depth and could not be reached by "Drift Working."

The Bristol Brick Company closed down their brick making industry in the St George area. The quarry was filled in and grassed over. Fussells closed down their roof tile industry. Their factory was near Crofts End Mission. The quarry was partly filled in, taken over by timber merchants. The Hollychrome Brick Company closed down their brick making industry. Their factory was between Fishponds and Speedwell. With all these industries closing down, it meant that their employees had to seek employment elsewhere. With so many people drifting away to other areas, it meant that the whole community was changing. People were keeping themselves to themselves, not mixing family with family as they did in earlier years. The motor car brought about a great change in community life. The workers were receiving a better standard of living, families were able to buy their own houses and housing conditions were far better than they were in earlier years. Television kept families at home more, washing machines made life easier for women, people were better clothed, employees were given paid holidays, making whole families independent of one another. The neighbourly spirit is still there, but the community spirit that once existed is now gone.

I very often wander around the areas where once the pits and quarries were in full production. The whole area is now very different. Where it was full of life, whole groups of people talking and joking with one another, it is now quiet; a new atmosphere is abroad, and only the ghosts of yesteryear are left.

Even the churches and chapels have been affected. Once upon a time churches and chapels were filled with people. There were marvellous church choirs, both adult and children's choirs that were a joy to listen to. Today all you can see is empty churches, overgrown with grass, and weeds are on the graves that used to be kept neat and tidy. Some churches have been demolished, houses and flats are being built on the ground where the church used to stand. Graves have been opened up, the bodies or remains have been moved elsewhere. The graves have then been filled in, allowing houses to be built over what was a graveyard.

Chapels are no longer attracting large attendances like they used to. So many of them have become dilapidated, crumbling away for the want of repair and paint. Yes, it is a far different community today. The people in earlier years loved their place of worship, and there was always a large number of volunteers ready to keep their chapel neat and tidy. They kept the grass short by cutting it mostly by using shears or scythe. They were a caring community.

I do not know if everything I have written down is relevant to what people want to know about those earlier years. Perhaps there are a few instances where I have been able to help. As you can tell by my phrasing, I have had only a council school education, but I think I have made myself understood.

Fred Moss, 1986, overlooking the playing fields at Speedwell School that used to be the site of the Colliery.